50 Quick Ways

More

CW00832224

By Mike Gershon

Text Copyright © 2016 Mike Gershon

All Rights Reserved

About the Author

Mike Gershon is known in the United Kingdom and beyond as an expert educationalist whose knowledge of teaching and learning is rooted in classroom practice. His online teaching tools have been viewed and downloaded more than 3.5 million times, making them some of the most popular of all time.

He is the author of over 80 books and guides covering different areas of teaching and learning. Some of Mike's bestsellers include books on assessment for learning, questioning, differentiation and outstanding teaching, as well as Growth Mindsets. You can train online with Mike, from anywhere in the world, at www.tes.com/institute/cpd-courses-teachers.

You can also find out more at www.mikegershon.com and www.gershongrowthmindsets.com, including about Mike's inspirational in-school training and student workshops.

Training and Consultancy

Mike offers a range of training and consultancy services covering all areas of teaching and learning, raising achievement and classroom practice. Examples of recent training events include:

- Assessment for Learning: Theory and Practice Keynote Address – Leigh Academies Trust Conference, London
- Growth Mindsets: Staff Training, Student Workshops and Speech to Parents – Longton Primary School, Preston
- Effective Questioning to Raise Achievement – Shireland Collegiate Academy, Birmingham

To find out more, visit www.mikegershon.com or www.gershongrowthmindsets.com or get in touch via mike@mikegershon.com

Other Works from the Same Author

Available to buy now on Amazon:

How to use Differentiation in the Classroom: The Complete Guide

How to use Assessment for Learning in the Classroom: The Complete Guide

How to use Bloom's Taxonomy in the Classroom: The Complete Guide

How to use Questioning in the Classroom: The Complete Guide

How to use Discussion in the Classroom: The Complete Guide

How to Manage Behaviour in the Classroom: The Complete Guide

How to Teach EAL Students in the Classroom: The Complete Guide

How to be an Outstanding Trainee Teacher: The Complete Guide

More Secondary Starters and Plenaries

Secondary Starters and Plenaries: History

Teach Now! History: Becoming a Great History Teacher

The Growth Mindset Pocketbook (with Professor Barry Hymer)

The Exams, Tests and Revision Pocketbook (from April 2016)

Also available to buy now on Amazon, the entire 'Quick 50' Series:

50 Quick and Brilliant Teaching Ideas

50 Quick and Brilliant Teaching Techniques

50 Quick and Easy Lesson Activities

50 Quick Ways to Help Your Students Secure A and B Grades at GCSE

50 Quick Ways to Help Your Students Think, Learn, and Use Their Brains Brilliantly

50 Quick Ways to Motivate and Engage Your Students

50 Quick Ways to Outstanding Teaching

50 Quick Ways to Perfect Behaviour Management

50 Quick and Brilliant Teaching Games

50 Quick and Easy Ways Leaders Can Prepare for Ofsted

50 Quick and Easy Ways to Outstanding Group Work

50 Quick and Easy Ways to Prepare for Ofsted

50 Quick Ways to Stretch and Challenge More-Able Students

50 Quick Ways to Create Independent Learners

50 Quick Ways to go from Good to Outstanding

50 Quick Ways to Support Less-Able Learners

And forthcoming in Summer 2016:

50 Quick Ways to Get Past 'I Don't Know'

50 Quick Ways to Start Your Lesson with a Bang!

50 Quick Ways to Improve Literacy Across the Curriculum

50 Quick Ways to Success with Life After Levels

50 Quick Ways to Improve Feedback and Marking

About the Series

The 'Quick 50' series was born out of a desire to provide teachers with practical, tried and tested ideas, activities, strategies and techniques which would help them to teach brilliant lessons, raise achievement and engage and inspire their students.

Every title in the series distils great teaching wisdom into fifty bite-sized chunks. These are easy to digest and easy to apply – perfect for the busy teacher who wants to develop their practice and support their students.

Acknowledgements

My thanks to all the staff and students I have worked with past and present, particularly those at Pimlico Academy and King Edward VI School, Bury St Edmunds. Thanks also to the teachers and teaching assistants who have attended my training sessions and who always offer great insights into what works in the classroom. Finally, thanks to Gordon at Kall Kwik for his design work and to Alison and Andy Metcalfe for providing a space in which to write.

Table of Contents

Introduction

All students need to have their thinking stretched. All students need a high level of challenge if they are to achieve their potential. For many, stretch and challenge comes through the main lesson activities, the content planned by the teacher, and the work which flows from both.

In any group of students, however, there will be those who are, at that point in time, more able than their peers. For these students, something extra is usually required. The stretch and challenge inherent in the main body of the lesson will not be enough to really push their thinking, their skills or their understanding.

In this book, I'll show you fifty different ways you can provide that something extra. Fifty different ways you can stretch and challenge your more-able students. Each of the ideas is presented in a ready-to-use form – but don't let that stop you from testing, adapting and modifying them to fit your teaching style and your students.

So without further ado, let us look at what we can do in the classroom to make great learning happen.

New Content Menu

01 New content means something else to think about. The challenge here is twofold. First, students have to spend time and effort understanding the new information. Second, they have to make sense of it in relation to what the lesson has already covered.

Offering a new content menu is a great way to liven up the process of stretching the thinking of more-able students.

Present a set of five options. Each one should represent additional content the student must research, explore and then summarise, ready to explain back to you. Invite the student to select one of the options, then point them to their research tools (books, a computer or a smartphone).

Further develop the idea by posing one or more questions which students have to answer in the course of their research. For example: How does the new content change your understanding of what we've done in the lesson so far?

Higher Level Content

02 The aim here is to challenge students by having them engage with content designed for older students. In some cases this means a greater level of complexity or abstraction. For example, a Year 10 English student being asked to read a poem usually left until Year 12.

In other cases, it means students having to look again at what constitutes success. For example, a Year 8 PE student being asked to attempt a skill usually reserved for GCSE courses.

When introducing higher level content, make a game out of it by writing the letters A and B on two scraps of paper, scrunching these up, and holding them behind your back, one in each hand. Invite students to choose a hand at random. Open it up to reveal the letter. Have two ideas ready for higher level content – one for A and one for B. Whichever letter is revealed, this is the content you should ask students to explore.

Expect the Unexpected

03 The unexpected is challenging because we cannot rely on doing what we have already done. By virtue of being unexpected, the situation demands that we think about our response and tailor it to deal with whatever is placed in front of us.

More-able students can often call on their existing skills and knowledge to deal easily with the main body of the lesson. Challenge them by throwing in unexpected tasks, questions and ideas, with the express intention of stopping them in their tracks and making them think more deeply. Here are three techniques you can use:

- When a more-able student is half-way through a task, throw in a new caveat or success criterion for them to meet.

- Pose an extension question which, on the surface at least, has nothing to do with the lesson. Challenge students to first develop an answer and then find a way of connecting this to the lesson topic.

- Use the 'What if…' question stem to pose questions which cause more-able students to go back and rethink their work. For example: What if I hadn't let you use any words to communicate your answer?

Problematize

04 Many more-able students grasp new ideas, information or skills quickly and easily. Think, for example, of the able Dance student who sees a new piece of choreography and can swiftly imitate it.

Problematizing means taking what is new and adding an additional layer to it – a layer of critical thinking. This compels more-able students to look again. We are helping them to see greater complexity than what they first observed; to develop a more nuanced, in-depth understanding.

In the example above, we might problematize the task by asking the student to come up with two divergent routines – one for a live audience and one for a video audience. Suddenly, the student has to step back and rethink what they initially grasped. While their first engagement with the skill was sound, our problematizing indicates that this is the first step in achieving mastery – not the last. Students are stretched and challenged as a result.

Prediction

05 Predictions stem from prior knowledge, existing understanding and the weighing up of possibilities. They are a form of judgement. When predicting, we make an assessment of what we think the future might be, based on the information we have available.

Due to the future's inherent unknowability, prediction is often tricky – particularly in areas where complexity reigns (such as economics, geopolitics or technological innovation). It is made trickier when we have to justify our predictions. Here, we not only have to work out what we think might happen, but justify it as well.

Asking more-able students to make and justify predictions allows you to stretch and challenge their thinking. Here are three techniques to try:

- Ask students at the beginning of the lesson to predict what the lesson will entail, based on the starter activity, and to justify this. Come back to them during the lesson and discuss whether and why they are revising their predictions.

- Give students limited information and ask them to use this to make and justify a prediction.

- Challenge students to make and justify predictions about real-life events connected to the topic (for example, the weather, politics, the result of a sports match).

Argue the Reverse

06 When a student knows what they think about a given topic, arguing the reverse is a challenge. First they need to look at matters from a different perspective, then they need to pick apart their own beliefs, in search of holes.

Here are some examples of when you can ask more-able students to argue the reverse:

- After they have created a written argument, such as an essay.

- After they have verbalised an argument in discussion. (Whole-class, group and paired discussions are all suitable.)

- If most of the class agree on a certain way of thinking. Here, you are asking your more-able students to play Devil's Advocate (for more on which, see later).

- After you have presented them with a specific argument. For example, a History teacher might put forward an argument about the Treaty of Versailles and then challenge a more-able student to argue the reverse.

- Before they go ahead with a practical endeavour. For example, before letting a student use a mortise and tenon joint in a DT lesson, you might ask them to argue the case for an alternative joint – just to ensure they fully understand the reasons behind their original choice.

Concept Mapping

07 Concepts are ideas. When we think, we rely on them. Along with categories, they form the bedrock of our thinking. Without concepts, we would be lost (only, we wouldn't know what lost meant!).

Concept mapping sees students taking a key concept and creating a map with this as the starting point. It can be in the form of a mind-map, or it can be vertical or horizontal in design. (Vertical – the key concept is written at the bottom of the page and everything maps upwards. Horizontal – the key concept is written at the left hand side of the page and everything maps rightwards).

To make concept mapping really challenging, ask students to include images, processes, people, places and facts, as well as other concepts, on their maps. Then, take things further by asking students to colour-code connections and/or themes. Finally, stretch student thinking by asking them to describe how their map would change if it was three-dimensional.

And, if you really want to stretch their thinking, ask them what would happen if the map became fourth dimensional (the fourth dimension being time).

When getting students started on a concept map you can specify the concept, provide a choice, or let them pick one themselves.

Conceptual Questioning

08 Conceptual questioning is abstract. This is because it revolves around concepts which, as we noted in the last entry, are ideas. And ideas, while referring to real things, don't exist physically themselves.

Conceptual questioning is challenging because students have to manipulate abstract ideas. They are compelled to analyse and examine some of the foundations on which their thinking rests. Here are some examples of conceptual questions, with (some of) the concepts highlighted:

- Were the Witches **right** to tell Macbeth of his future?

- What if we could speed up and slow down **natural selection**?

- Why is only one of these pictures a **masterpiece**?

- How does a business know if it thinks about **value** in the same way as its customers?

- Is it ever OK for friends to **lie** to each other?

The concepts relevant to your students will vary depending on what area of the curriculum you are teaching. Some concepts come up again and again (ethical ones such as right and wrong being an obvious example), while other concepts have different meanings in different settings (consider change in the context of Geology and Food Technology).

Concept Exploration

09 Staying on the topic of concepts, a fruitful way to stretch and challenge student thinking is by inviting them to explore concepts in more depth than the rest of the class.

For example, in a lesson looking at the concept of persuasive writing, we might provide more-able students with a chance to explore this idea in greater detail.

As the rest of the class continue with the main task, we could present more-able students with examples of persuasive writing from three different eras – an advert from the 1960s, one from the 1980s and one from the 2000s, for example – and ask them to compare and contrast these, before answering the question: Do you think persuasive writing has stayed the same over time?

Here, the aim is push more-able students to deepen their understanding of the concept. Contrast and comparison activities are always good for this. They develop discrimination by asking students to examine separate items in relation to one another.

Cross-Examination

10 Usually reserved for the courtroom, a cross-examination challenges students to think on their feet and defend their views.

You can cross-examine more-able students at any time – during a task, during discussion, as part of the plenary, or even when you see them in the corridor.

To cross-examine effectively, select your topic (usually the lesson topic) and ask students what they think. Then, begin chipping away at their answer. Play the role of a prosecutor in a courtroom. Your aim is to find out if what the student said really is the truth.

Some cross-examination questions include:

- Why do you think that?

- Yes, but have you considered...?

- But what if...happened?

- What if someone disagreed with you?

- Can you prove that?

In one sense, the stretch and challenge here comes from the process as much as the end result. A student who regularly has their ideas cross-examined by the teacher regularly gets to go through the process of defending, developing and refining their thinking.

Concept Explanation

11 Explaining a concept sounds easy...at first. What is courage? Well, courage is what you have when you are brave. Yes, but what is it? Where can I find it? Well, you can't find courage, but you can see it. Can you show me? Err, it's a bit difficult to show you right now. But I thought you knew what courage was? I do, I do, but...

Asking more-able students to explain key concepts to you means asking them to offer a detailed description of an idea. While they may have good intuitive understanding of ideas – meaning they can rely on them when thinking, working and doing practical things – this will not always translate into the ability to articulate the meaning of a concept.

And that is why explaining a concept is a challenge! You are asking students to go back to something on which they rely and explain it from scratch.

Further increase the level of challenge by stating an audience for the explanation – such as an alien or a group of younger students.

Assess This!

12 Assessment is at the top of Bloom's Taxonomy. It is one of the more challenging cognitive skills. Asking more-able students to assess something means asking them to stretch their thinking by making and defending judgements.

You can ask students to assess all sorts:

- Their work

- Model work

- Their peer's work

- Work you have created (good or bad) for the purpose of the exercise

- An argument

- A decision or choice

- A set of options

- A way of doing something (for example, assess this way of moving the ball from the back of the court to the front)

- Possible answers to a question

- The quality of a question

Change the level of challenge by giving students more or less support as they make their assessments. The more support you give, the easier the task becomes.

Practice Testing

13 Practice testing involves practising for a real test. For example:

- Taking a mock exam paper

- Practising exam-style questions

- Planning possible answers to exam-style questions

- Creating and then using a set of flashcards

- Writing model answers to exam questions

- Writing and then taking exam-style questions

For greatest impact, practice testing should be low stakes. This emphasises that it is a learning opportunity, not a zero-sum game.

Practice testing is challenging in itself. You can increase the level of challenge by making the practice questions harder or by raising the bar on what you expect from student responses. For example, you might explain that you are less interested in whether the student scores 90% or 100% and more interested in the care with which they formulate their answers.

Beat the Teacher

14 A classic game with many variations. The concept is simple: the student has to find a way to beat the teacher. To do this, they will have to push themselves, thinking more deeply and working harder as a result.

Here are five variations on the theme:

- Challenge a more-able student to come up with a question connected to the topic to which they know the answer but which you don't.

- Challenge a more-able student to perform a skill or derivation of a skill more successfully than you can (most appropriate in practical subjects).

- Challenge a more-able student to write a five question quiz based on the topic. They should also come up with the answers, before using the quiz to try to beat you.

- Challenge a more-able student to come up with a question connected to the topic to which neither you nor they know the answer.

- Develop the previous point by then engaging in a 'research race' to discover the answer.

Semantic Interrogation

15 This is the process through which we attribute meaning to things. It centres on asking the question: 'why?'

For example, our partner is leaving the house. As they exit, they call back: 'Make sure the windows are fully closed. Don't leave any on the safety lock.' For a moment, as the door slams, we stand and wonder why they have made this bizarre statement. Then, in an act of semantic interrogation, we find a way to give meaning to the utterance.

Today is the first Tuesday of the month. The window cleaner is due. If the windows are on safety, some suds can squeeze through. Hence **why** we need to check that every window is fully closed.

Challenge more-able students by asking them to engage in semantic interrogation. Ask them questions such as:

- Yes, but why is this the case?
- Why might this be true?
- What is the reason behind this?
- Why should someone do it that way and not this way?
- Why is there a connection between these two things?

Topic Monologue

16 A monologue is a dramatic device in which the actor delivers an extended piece of speech. You can adapt this technique to stretch and challenge students in your classroom.

Invite a more-able student to write their own monologue. That is, an extended piece of them talking, based on the topic of study. Explain that the monologue does not have to be a speech – it is simply them speaking, as if to an audience. However, indicate that the monologue does need to keep the audience engaged. The student needs to think about how they maintain interest and enthusiasm while also getting across key information about the topic.

When the monologue has been written, invite the student to deliver it to you. Increase the level of challenge by making a rough line graph indicating how interested and engaged you feel (as the audience). Make sure the student can see this as they speak – if it appears you are losing interest they will soon realise and have to make immediate changes to compensate!

Start/End

17 Provide more-able students with the start and end of something before leaving them to work out the middle. Here are five examples:

- A Dance teacher gives their student the start and the end of a piece of choreography.

- A PE teacher gives their student the start and end of a gymnastics routine.

- A History teacher gives their student the start and end of an essay.

- A Year 6 teacher gives their student the start and end of a story.

- A Year 5 teacher gives their student the start and end (solution) of a problem.

In each case, the student's challenge is to use the limited information they have as a jumping off point.

The level of challenge can be increased by providing caveats. For example, the PE teacher might specify three things which need to happen in between the start and end of the gymnastics routine.

Refine the Process

18 Students use processes throughout their time in the classroom. A process is any kind of procedure, or way of doing things, a student calls on to help create a piece of work, answer a question or respond to a task.

For example: the process of sequencing ideas before writing an essay; the process of visualising a long jump before doing the jump for real; the process of checking the accuracy of your results before analysing them for patterns and trends.

More-able students are often sufficiently confident with the processes on which they rely that they give little active thought to them. However, processes can always be refined.

You can challenge these students by asking them to do just this – refine the processes on which their thought, actions or work rest.

For example, a History teacher might ask a student to make their process of sequencing ideas more flexible, so that they can better respond to the demands of different questions. Or, a Chemistry teacher might ask a student to record their data twice in a double-entry system so they can improve the reliability of their accuracy checking.

Process Feedback

19 As well as asking students to focus specifically on refining a process, we can provide more general process feedback. This involves telling students what they have done well, in terms of processes, and what they could do to improve. For example:

"Jack, I can see from this drawing that you have spent time sketching out how you want the foreground to look. This is good as it has led to a final image which is complex and engaging. Next time, I'd like you to use the same process for the background as well."

Here, the process is sketching out ideas in advance. Jack has used this to create a better end product when it comes to the foreground of the image. In the future, he could do the same for all parts of his image.

Process feedback helps more-able students start to see their skills, knowledge and understanding as a permanent work-in-progress. Continuous improvement then becomes the challenge.

Process Questioning

20 A complement to process feedback is process questioning. Here, we question students about the processes they are using, or which they have used, to create a piece of work or complete a certain task.

For example:

- 'Saira, what made you decide to use the cubes to help you check the calculations?'

Or:

- 'Amy, how would you explain to Nathan how you planned your story?'

When working with more-able students, the aim is to get them to reflect on the processes they have used. This can be an end in itself, promoting metacognition and the development of thinking. Or, it can be the prelude to a discussion between you and the student. In the latter case, this could see the two of you assessing the efficacy of different processes or weighing up the pros and cons of the student changing their approach.

Try It This Way – Then Tell Me About It

21 There's more than one way to skin a cat. And there's nearly always more than one way to answer a question, complete a task or make use of a skill.

Challenge your more-able students when they have finished the main activity by asking them to do whatever they have done in a different way, specified by you. Then, ask them to tell you about how they got on – and to compare this with their first attempt.

Here's an example:

In a Key Stage Three Maths lesson the teacher notices that two of the more-able students have been taught a particular method for long division. When they have completed the practice calculations, the teacher invites them up to the front and shows them both an alternative method. She then challenges them to try using this on a new set of sums, before coming back to the front to discuss the results.

Expert Practice

22 Experts prepare. In fact, they over-prepare. This means that when they come to do a thing for real, they can rely on powerful long-term memories of how to do the thing in question.

In a physical discipline such as rugby or ballet, these memories are muscular as well as cognitive. In a mental discipline such as essay writing, they are mostly the latter (though pen/keyboard manipulation is included as well, albeit in a limited sense).

Challenge your more-able students by explaining the virtues of practice to them and how this creates the path to expertise. Then, ask them to identify a specific skill they need to practice to get closer to becoming an expert.

Finally, give them space in which to practice this skill.

Encourage excessive repetition allied to active engagement (cognitive, physical or a mixture depending on the skill) with the task in hand. Ask students to think about how they can get better on each occasion. Finally, and when they have done their practice, invite them to talk you through or show you the results.

Weakness Practice

23 Some more-able students prefer to focus on their strengths while ignoring their weaknesses. For these students, an excellent challenge comes in the form of weakness practice.

Either on your own or in discussion with your student, identify an area where they have weaknesses. For example, a more-able Food Technology student may excel in following recipes but struggle when it comes to thinking creatively.

Having done this, challenge the student in question to focus their energies on practising to overcome their weakness. In the example above, the student would focus on embellishing, developing and tweaking the recipes the teacher gives them. The teacher would make it clear that this is what they will look at and assess, for the moment, with other things temporarily put to one side.

Develop the technique by asking the student to talk you through how their practice has led them to improve. This sees them reflecting on the process and articulating their understanding of what has happened.

Flooding

24 What does a flooded town look like?

That's the visual metaphor for flooding as a technique. Our aim is to give more-able students so much information, or so much to do, that they are momentarily flooded. In this state of temporary disorientation they will have to think quickly and carefully about what they can do to regain equilibrium. Here are three examples of flooding:

- Set the class a task accompanied by three success criteria. Give more-able students a further four success criteria and explain they have the same length of time as everybody else to complete their work.

- Pose a question to the class, provide some research materials and indicate how long students have to develop an answer. As students get started, pose a further two questions to your more-able students and indicate that you would like an answer to these, as well as the original question, in the time specified.

- Divide the class into pairs. Give each pair three sources to analyse, connected to the topic. Provide any pair containing a more-able student with an additional three sources to analyse in the time allowed.

Caveats

25 We've mentioned caveats a number of times already, in conjunction with other techniques. We can also think about them as a tool in their own right.

A caveat is any additional expectation you place on a student when they are completing a task. Caveats increase the level of challenge because they compel students to think, work and act in certain ways – ways they might otherwise have avoided or dismissed.

You can challenge more-able students by providing caveats planned specifically for them. These can be delivered at the start of a task, or mid-way through.

Here are some examples:

- You may only use short sentences in this particular speech.
- You're not allowed to touch the ball more than twice at a time during this match.
- You must include at least five shades of green in your painting.
- Your sonnet must follow an ABAB ABAB ABBA BB structure.
- Your story must include at least one unexpected twist.

Break It Down

26 Breaking information down into separate sections requires students to use their skills of analysis. You can challenge more-able students by asking them to do this with new information they have learned during the lesson.

For example, in a French lesson where students have been learning a new set of words, the teacher could challenge more-able students to divide these words up into a series of categories. At this point, you can vary the extent of the challenge. To keep things simple, tell the students in question what categories you would like them to use. To make things harder, invite them to identify suitable categories themselves.

Another 'Break It Down' technique involves asking students to categorise information from a series of lessons. For example, a Geography teacher might ask a more-able student to break down all the keywords learned during a term into a Venn diagram covering human and physical geography.

Increased Complexity

27 Increasing the level of complexity increases the level of challenge by making greater demands on students' working memory. With more to think about, students have to attend more closely to what they are doing. In addition, they may find the usual processes on which they rely to be less efficacious than usual – because the increased level of complexity overwhelms them. This means students have to go back and think again about how to tackle the task.

Here are five ways you can increase the level of complexity for more-able students:

- Give more-able students an additional sub-task they have to complete, on top of the main activity.

- Constrain more-able students by ruling something out. For example: 'You're not allowed to use your calculator for these questions.'

- Give more-able students extra information than their peers.

- Ask more-able students to do the same task as the rest of the class, but with an additional element. For example, while the rest of the class has to compare worship in two religions, more-able students must compare it across three.

- Provide extra success criteria. This becomes especially complex if the criteria are highly specific. For example (in rugby), I want to see at least two cut-out passes in the next three phases of play.

Complex Questioning

28 Here are some examples of relatively simple questions:

- What might Churchill have felt like at the end of the war?

- How can we find the area of this shape?

- What might happen when we mix the chemicals?

And here are the same questions made more complex:

- What might Churchill have felt like as the war drew to a close – and is this of any interest to historians, or are the emotions and feelings of major historical figures irrelevant when compared to the wider picture?

- How can we find the area of this shape with a method we could then apply to find the area of any other shape – and would this method be the only one possible, or one among many?

- What might happen when we mix the chemicals and how might this be influenced by changes in temperature, changes in the quantity of chemicals mixed and changes in the atmospheric conditions?

Note in each case how the complexity puts an intellectual onus onto the student, stretching their thinking. Equally, note that the complexity of the questions is connected to both the topic and the age of the student.

Preparation Guidelines

29 If you are teaching a course which leads to an exam – or if you are teaching a unit which concludes with an assessment – you can challenge more-able students by asking them to create preparation guidelines.

These are guidelines which could be given to a prospective student, explaining in detail everything they need to know, understand and be able to do to be sufficiently prepared for the exam or assessment.

The challenge stems from students having to think at length about all they have learnt, as well as how this connects to the way in which their learning will be assessed.

You can increase the level of challenge by specifying who the prospective students are and what prior knowledge they will bring. Another option is to limit the number of words students can use in their guidelines, meaning they have to think carefully about how to convey the information through images.

If Questions

30 The word 'if' signals a hypothetical. If this happens, then that will happen. If I want to go out tomorrow night, then I need to do my homework during the day. If Arsenal win the league this year, then I'll be very happy.

The challenge with hypotheticals is that they are inherently uncertain. By posing questions to students constructed in this form, you are asking them to think critically and creatively, to speculate and to reason. Here are some examples:

- If you had to introduce a new character into the story, where would you do it and why?

- If we had used a different solution, then what might have happened? Why?

- If human rights were suspended whenever the country was at war, what might be the consequences for political decision-making?

- If we adopt pressing tactics in the first-half, how might it play out across the game as a whole?

- If Catherine of Aragon had given birth to a son, how might Henry's reign have been different?

Devil's Advocate

31 Playing Devil's Advocate means doing one of two things:

- Taking up an unlikely, hard-to-defend or uncommon position and then defending this as if you truly believed it.

- Consistently arguing against whatever the student puts forward, therefore continually putting the onus onto them to defend and support their views.

In both cases, the aim is to make students work harder, to think more carefully about their ideas, views or arguments, and to think more critically about positions they may have ignored or dismissed.

You can play Devil's Advocate at almost any point in the lesson to stretch and challenge the thinking of your more-able students. However, I would suggest it is at its most effective when students have spent some time developing their ideas. For example, after a discussion, during a discussion or mid-way through an extended task.

In these situations, students have more to defend. This means taking on the role of Devil's Advocate is likely to result in a more engaged – and impassioned! – debate.

A Different Voice

32 Ask students to think, write, create, act or do something in a different voice.

By different voice we mean that students have to take on someone else's perspective. Here are some examples:

- Can you replay the point but this time take on the role of someone who only ever plays serve and volley?

- Can you rewrite your answer from the perspective of a government minister?

- Can you create a different image? This time, work from the point of view of someone who dislikes colour.

- Read the monologue again, but this time imagine the character is reluctant to share their story with the audience.

- Develop a different design from the perspective of someone who doesn't want the product to be successful.

Make It Better

33 Some more-able students struggle to see the value in trying to make their work better. For them, finishing can be the aim, rather than making something the best it can be.

When working with these students, you can stretch and challenge them simply by asking them to improve the quality of their work as soon as they finish it. Because these students may struggle, at first, to understand how to do this, you should provide guidance by highlighting specific areas on which they could focus. For example:

- 'Thanks, Maryam. Now I'd like you to go back and rewrite the third, fourth and fifth paragraphs so they include more relevant examples.'

- 'Thanks, David. Can you take another look at questions 2, 7 and 9? I'd like to see you express your working out more clearly so it's easier for me to follow the process you used to get your answer. When you've done, call me over and talk me through it.'

- 'Thanks, Tasha. I'd like you to go back and practise the first part of the routine. I can see what you're trying to do, but I want to see more control over the position of your arms and legs.'

Make It Worse

34 This seems perverse! Why would you want a student to make their work worse?

Well, if a student fully understands what would make something worse, then they have a sound understanding of what makes something good. One side sheds light on the other.

Here are three examples of what the technique looks like in practice:

- Go back through your mock exam paper and identify three places where doing one thing worse would lose you at least five marks. Use the mark-scheme to help you.

- If you were going to redo this essay so that it was of an inferior standard, what three specific changes would you make? For each one, write a paragraph explaining why this would make the essay worse.

- Take another look at your leaflet. What two changes would have the biggest negative impact? Why would these changes make it less likely that your leaflet met the success criteria?

Shoe Box Tombola

35 This is a fun way to deliver extension questions and tasks.

Take a shoe box and cover it in shiny paper. Create a set of generic extension questions and/or tasks. Write each of these on a slip of paper. Fold the slips and place them in the box.

When a more-able student has completed the main activity, bring out the shoe box and explain that their extension task/question is a lucky dip. They need to root around in the tombola and select one of the slips of paper at random. Whatever is written on there is the question or task they need to complete.

This technique adds an element of fun and excitement to extension questions/tasks.

If you are unsure about how to come up with generic questions/tasks, try using a list of keywords from the top two levels of Bloom's taxonomy (synthesis and evaluation). Another option is to include a slip of paper which reads: 'Write your own extension question – then answer it and use it to test the teacher.'

Write Your Own Extension

36 And this is such a good technique that it deserves its own entry – as well as being part of Shoe Box Tombola.

Asking students to write their own extension questions is challenging. They need to think about what they have learned thus far in the lesson, what they know and what sort of question would be sufficiently difficult to stretch them beyond their current understanding.

When flipping things round and asking students to develop their own extension question, be aware that you might need to offer some support, at least initially. This can include:

- Providing possible question stems

- Defining the subject of the extension question

- Giving a model question as an example

- Providing possible keywords (e.g. command words such as outline, describe, assess)

- Reminding students of previous extension questions you've posed to them

Off-Topic

37 Sometimes it's good to go completely off-topic. If a more-able student has a particular interest connected to the subject but not to the present topic, you can make use of this by letting them explore it when they have finished the main activity.

Here are some examples of how it can work:

- OK Jimmy, if you've finished the work on forces I'll give you five minutes to investigate astronomy while the rest of the class catch up.

- Well done, Rashid – why don't you grab a textbook and have a look at the War of the Roses while everyone else is finishing up their WW1 work.

- Good job, Claudia – take five minutes to practice your step-overs while the group keep working on their short passing.

In each case the challenge is essentially self-directed. Jimmy, Rashid and Claudia have their own interests. These cannot be pursued in the lesson until the teacher gives the say-so. When they do, however, the students can start stretching themselves by following up on their personal goals.

Additional Success Criteria

38 We've mentioned this idea in passing on a couple of occasions, and it has obvious links to the earlier entry on Caveats. It's another technique worthy of a separate treatment, though.

When providing more-able students with additional success criteria, the aim is to increase the level of challenge they face when completing the main activity. Here, we are asking them to do the same as the rest of the class, plus something extra. It's fairly easy to come up with additional success criteria that stretch student thinking – and even to do it on the hoof. Nonetheless, here are some approaches you might like to try:

- Throw it over to the student by asking them to come up with a challenging extra success criterion.

- Use a word prefixed by 're' as the subject of your extra criterion: redo, revisit, revise, rewrite, reimagine.

- Include an extra criterion that asks the student to do something highly specific or technical.

- Pose an additional criterion which asks the student to connect the current task to another area of the curriculum.

Greater Detail/Depth

39 Asking more-able students to go into greater detail or depth means asking them to demonstrate a greater stock of knowledge and understanding. It also indicates that this is of value in and of itself – not just as a means to an end (such as scoring marks or getting a certain grade).

One of the difficulties students face here is that they do not always understand exactly what greater detail/depth means.

Help them over this hurdle by specifying what you want to see when you talk about greater detail or depth:

- I'd like to see more explanation of the key terms on your poster – imagine it was going into a magazine and that the reader expects to be provided with extensive information.

- Your first two paragraphs are quite vague. I'd like to see them rewritten with a focus on detail. Make sure the reader knows exactly what the essay is about by the time they've read those paragraphs.

- Your tactical plan doesn't specify what the team will do if the opposition score early. I'd like you to add this extra layer of detail, please.

Broadcast It

40 Modern technology means creating videos and audio files is easy. Most students now have smartphones. They can use these to create pieces of media teaching, explaining or demonstrating key aspects of their learning.

Take advantage of this fact by using it to challenge your more-able students. Here are some examples of how to do it:

- Create a 30-second video explaining the three most difficult ideas we've looked at this term – for an audience who know nothing about the topic.

- Create a 60-second video showing five different ways to pass the ball from easiest to most difficult.

- Create a 90-second audio file of an imaginary debate between Kissinger and Nixon on the topic of the Vietnam War.

- Create a 60-second voiceover for an advert alerting students to the risks of drugs. Your voiceover should be persuasive and informative.

- Create a 60-second video demonstrating three different ways to solve an equation, with a 10-second summary at the end stating which is best and why.

Read Ahead

41 If your more-able students complete their work before their peers, a simple way to stretch and challenge them is by inviting them to read ahead. Part of the challenge is that they encounter new information without the support of the teacher and a series of planned activities.

When specifying what you would like them to read about, bear in mind that this doesn't necessarily have to be the next thing you intend to focus on in your lessons. For example, you might invite students to read ahead about a topic they will be studying in a month's time. Or, you might ask them to read ahead on the current topic, even though your sequence of lessons is coming to an end.

These two examples demonstrate there is plenty of flexibility when it comes to reading ahead. Whatever you ask students to do, they will be taking in more information and further developing their understanding.

Another option is to cut out and laminate interesting/relevant newspaper and magazine articles. Keep these in your room and you will always have them on hand for students to read, as an alternative.

Read Above

42 Following on from the previous entry, why not challenge more-able students to read something usually reserved for older students?

Reading above your current level of understanding is an excellent way to move beyond what you currently know. Sometimes, this means giving students texts with which they will struggle. This is a good thing – though you may need to explain to your students why this is the case.

For example, a GCSE Psychology teacher might print off an academic paper and give this to one of their more-able students. 'Whenever you finish the main activity, dig this out of your folder and read a bit more of it,' they might say to their student.

Initially, the student will almost certainly struggle. Academic papers are usually dense, written for a specialised audience and contain technical language. The teacher tells the student about this, but insists they keep going anyway. Through the process they'll start to learn how to unpick some of these problem areas. And they'll also learn about persisting in the face of adversity.

Serial Questioning

43 This is where we pose a series of questions to a student or group of students, with all the questions connected to the topic of discussion.

When using serial questioning to stretch and challenge the more-able, our aim is to push their thinking, not letting them off the hook or giving them an easy ride. You can plan a series of questions or develop them on the go. Either way, it involves the teacher posing an initial question and not leaving until they have followed up with a fair few more (perhaps seven or eight).

Here's an example of a series of questions posed to a more-able GCSE Sociology student (with student responses left to your imagination):

- So do you think social class is still relevant today?

- But how easy is it to make accurate comparisons over time?

- Doesn't social class get in the way though, because it stops us focussing on gender and ethnicity?

- Is it really possible to focus on all three at the same time? How?

- True, but what if an individual decides to define their own identity?

- So what happens if a researcher says someone is working-class, because of their income, but they define themselves as middle-class?

- Would sociology be possible without any big categories at all?

- If there are all these problems with using social class, why does it remain so popular among sociologists?

Plan a Lesson

44 As we know, lesson planning can be challenging. Use this fact to stretch the thinking of your more-able students by asking them to plan a lesson based on their learning.

In doing this, students will have to think carefully about what they know, how well they understand it and how to present this in a way that is accessible and challenging for an audience of their peers (or younger students).

When setting a lesson planning task or extension, specify who the audience is and whether there are any caveats attached to the task, for example:

- The lesson must include at least two interactive elements.

- Your lesson should not contain any activities we've used today.

- The lesson should get progressively more challenging.

- Your lesson should contain at least one practice exam question.

- The lesson must centre on a big, engaging question.

Trial and Error

45 Trial and error is one of the most important ways in which we learn. Some more-able students are reluctant to use the approach, however, because they fear getting things wrong. Often, this is because they have developed a mindset in which they equate their sense of self with 'being clever' or 'always getting things right.'

Asking these students to use trial and error means challenging them to think differently.

This stretches them while also providing an insight into an approach they can start to apply in all areas of their learning.

You can ask students to use trial and error in most settings. Here are some examples:

- I'll only mark the answers if I can see the working out.

- I expect to see at least three first attempts before the finished product.

- I don't want a perfect piece of work, I want a piece of work that has been improved – and I want you to show me the improvements.

Impossible Problems

46 Some problems are impossible. Or, at least, they appear to be so at the moment.

Building a collection of impossible problems means having a cache on which you can call to stretch and challenge your more-able students. You can find plenty online by searching for:

- Impossible problems

- Philosophical problems

- Brainteasers

- Logic puzzles

- Mindbenders Puzzles

Copy and paste a selection of these into a Word file, along with the answers. Print this off and store it somewhere in your classroom. When a more-able student finishes the main activity, take out your Impossible Problems File, flick through and select one with which to challenge them.

Over time, this can be built up into a game, with you and your students taking on the dramatic roles of problem-setter and problem-solver.

As the problems we are talking about are of the impossible variety, don't be surprised if students need to keep working at them over the course of a few lessons.

Repeat: Sharper, Quicker

47 Doing something more sharply and more quickly means upping the ante. You don't have as much time to think, but you also need to do what you've done already with a higher degree of skill and accuracy.

For these reasons, asking more-able students to repeat something sharper and quicker is a challenge. Here are some examples:

- Sid, I now want you to try this 6-mark question. I'm going to give you one minute less than last time, and I want to see you aiming for six marks rather than five.

- Ashleigh, I want you to summarise the key findings of your experiment in the next two minutes – and I want the summary to focus exclusively on the numerical data.

- Mo, I want you to keep practising the forward defensive, but we're going to speed up the bowling machine. I also want to see less of a gate between your bat and pad.

Big Questions

48 Big questions require big thinking.

- What is the meaning of life?

- Does evolution disprove the existence of God?

- When does telling the truth become dangerous?

- How much freedom is enough?

- Is it OK to grow human organs in a laboratory?

Posing these kinds of questions to more-able students means giving them plenty of space in which to think. You can throw the questions out as extensions to the main activity, pose them at the start of the lesson and return to students as the session progresses, or leave students to think about them for a few lessons.

Another option is to create a sheet of big questions, print this off and give it to more-able students to stick in the back of their books. Then, whenever they have a free moment, invite them to scrutinise the sheet and to select one question they would like to think about and discuss with you or a peer.

Peer Teaching

49 Asking more-able students to teach their peers means asking them to reformulate their knowledge and understanding so as to make it comprehensible for an audience. In the process all students benefit.

Here are some examples of the approach in action:

- Misha, I'd like you to go around the room and find out who's struggling with applying the formula. Take your book with you and use it to teach them how to get it right.

- Darryl, I can see that Tom and Ed are finding it difficult to rank the sources from most to least important. Head over there and talk them through your ranking. Make sure you explain to them how you came to your decision, then see if you can help them do the same.

- Claire, why don't you go and work with Sam's group? They're finding it tough to give the text enough life. Talk them through some of the techniques you've used to engage the audience with Brecht's words.

Verbal Feedback

50 Our final way to stretch and challenge more-able students is the familiar technique of verbal feedback. This sees the teacher delivering feedback to students during the lesson and using this to direct their thinking and effort.

Verbal feedback can be particularly challenging for more-able students when:

- You focus on mistakes, using this as an opportunity to discuss why the mistakes happened and what can be learned from them.

- You provide students with a target and a limited period of time in which to implement it. For example, five minutes. When the five minutes are up, you should return to the student to see how they have done.

- It encourages them to think more critically about their work or to try taking a different approach from the one they usually favour.

- It comes in the form of a rhetorical question the student has to consider after you leave. For example: Who's to say that is the only way this could be tackled?

- It makes the activity more ambiguous. Students then have to navigate their way through the uncertainty your feedback has created.

And with that, we draw to a close. All that's left for me to say is that I hope you have found the ideas useful and good luck in stretching and challenging the thinking of your more-able students. I'm sure you'll do a great job.

A Brief Request

If you have found this book useful I would be delighted if you could leave a review on Amazon to let others know.

If you have any thoughts or comments, or if you have an idea for a new book in the series you would like me to write, please don't hesitate to get in touch at mike@mikegershon.com.

Finally, don't forget that you can download all my teaching and learning resources for **FREE** at www.mikegershon.com and www.gershongrowthmindsets.com

.

Printed in Great Britain
by Amazon